Western Shores

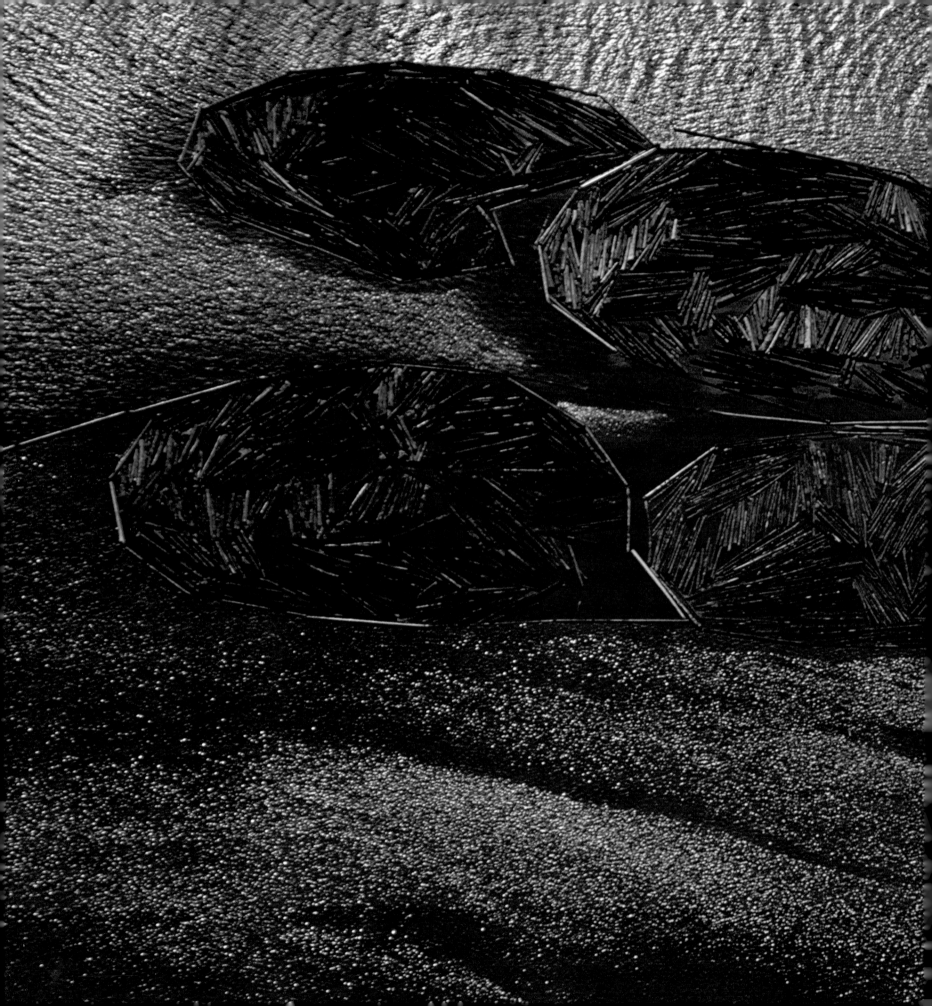

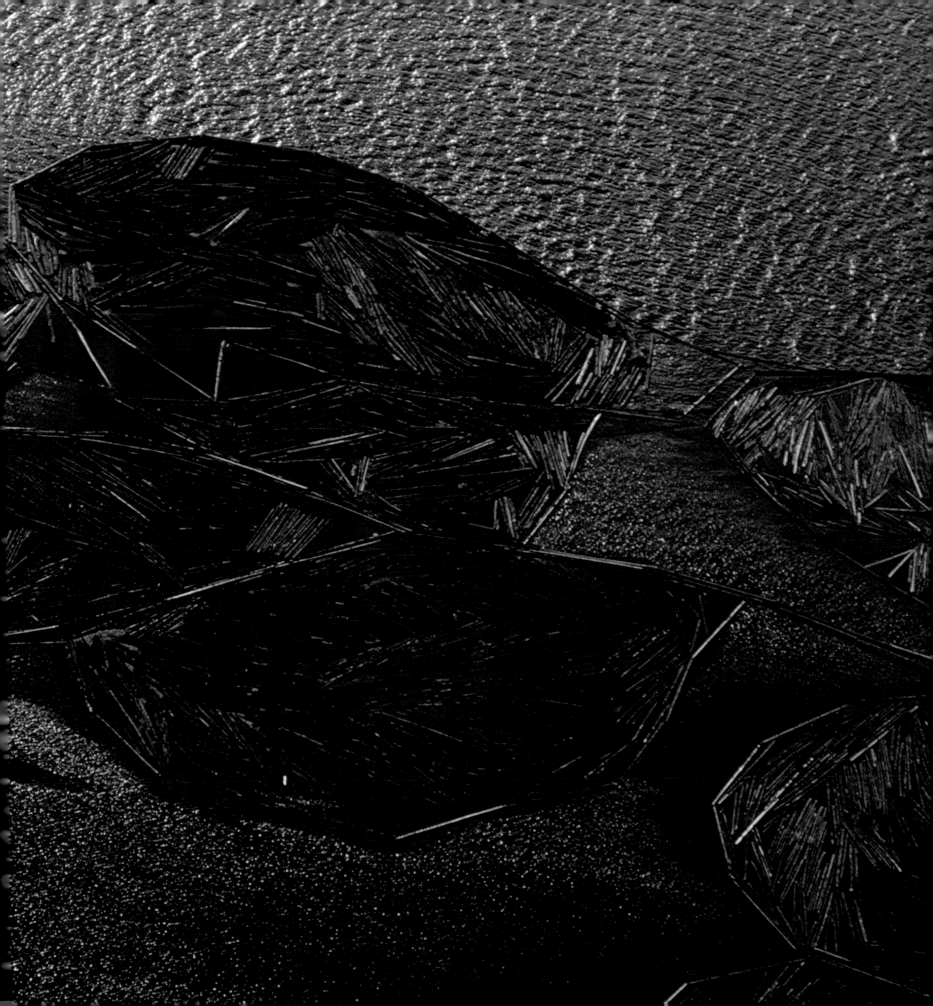

Contents

To the Mermaid

1

The Most Ancient Sound

One feels eternity on these shores;
mountains rising from the bowels of planet Earth,
waves sounding in endless chorus,
trees reaching for infinity.
Creatures thrive at the edge of the sea.
We are guardians of eternity.

Sixteen thousand miles of saltwater shoreline; part water-wilderness, part coastal metropolis. Awesome, lonely, congested, concerned – the British Columbia coast. Islets hiding behind the lowest, littlest clouds. In the mist, yellow, green, black on the near shore, dulling and blending into the horizon which the rainy day brings so nearby. Dark fjord walls, tufted silhouettes at water's edge. A billion reflections on leeward waters.

And there are voices in the air. Voices which flow from widely divergent life-styles, and respond to many different imperatives. As one listens to these voices one senses the spectrum of elements that comprise this coast. There is Alfie Collinson, the Indian who went back to a deserted village, sat in the pit of a roofless longhouse and fell back in time: "I was just gone." He came away determined to re-establish a personal relationship to his land, his heritage. There is Hap Kearns, the contractor who helped carve a modern town out of a stubborn wilderness – roads, schools, sewage plant, and now a swimming pool. "Couldn't have done without the challenge of building here – it was tough." And there is Murray Newman, the biologist who has brought sea-life from the coast's waters into an aquarium in Vancouver, so that city people can see killer whales and salmon and sea urchins and come to appreciate that "they are worth something in each of *our* lives."

And there is Stuart Holland, the geologist who remembers the year he did field studies for an oil company in Alberta. "I couldn't get back to B.C. fast enough. The prairies are so flat. There's nothing to see except a great bowl of sky. You look out there, and there's the horizon – just that. No outcrop at all, except along the valleys. Coming back, I could smell the coast when I got to Hope. The rotting organic mud, the burning slash – it's that, combined with the sea, that creates something indescribable. Even today coming over the hump, fifty miles from the coastline, everything just wells up inside of me. My whole boyhood on English Bay, all my beginnings. This is what I am. A product of having grown up, lived, and worked in British Columbia. There isn't any other place in Canada that has a coastline like British Columbia."

Stuart has given more than forty years to deciphering and writing about the four-and-a-half-billion-year history of this coast. Although now retired from the Department of Mines and Petroleum Resources, he's hardly lost his interest.

"The biggest surprise for most people if they'd go up one of these uninhabited fjords would be that they couldn't find a place to step off the boat onto land. The land rises so damned steeply, about like that." His hand jabs straight up. "You couldn't put an anchor down and catch bottom. There's no anchorage for miles and miles. Even if you have a small boat you could put up on a beach, there's no beaches."

He speaks of how the raw material of the coast was formed. At times, the magma rose directly from the earth's hot core and cooled rapidly into black columns of basalt. At times the molten flow was blocked by the formations above, and it cooled slowly into granite. The layers contracted and shifted as they cooled, and responded to new forces by lifting and twisting and shearing along the weakest beds. The shoreline of today is but an instant in the continuing cycle of its lowering and destruction, its re-elevation and erosion. It began to take on its present character in the cretaceous age, about one hundred million years ago. High mountains on the mainland and the island belt probably developed by the end of the tertiary – twenty million years ago. It was more the things that happened to the rocks, rather than the nature of the rocks, that counted. Granite, quartz diorite, and volcanic rocks reacted almost identically to the million-year-long ice age that ended just ten thousand years ago. Stuart's words carry one back into an era no man witnessed.

"It was really very quiet. The sound of time was rain and snow and the odd crunch. Erosion doesn't sound like a fellow rasping a piece of metal, but the ice is doing much the same thing. It's got a whole bunch of teeth. The rocks it pushes along are like cutting tools, and the glaciers are scouring out the valleys as they advance and recede. If ten thousand feet of the ice had been sitting on the Sierra of California, as it did here during the glacial age, their coast ranges would have been sitting offshore, as does our Vancouver Island, their great valley would have been flooded, like our Gulf of Georgia, and their coast would have been submerged and rising from the sea, as ours is today. . . ."

How did life come to these rocky shores? Biologist Bristol Foster, head of the British Columbia ecological reserve system, has speculated on this question. The saltchuck plays outside his home at Victoria's Ten Mile Point. "As I lie in bed at night I can hear the water. Sometimes it's roaring, sometimes it's *gurgling* . . . even when it's dead calm, there's always at least a gurgle. And I think before there was any life there must have been waves and gurgles. Along with the roar of volcanoes, it must be the most ancient sound.

"Then came the *tchika-tchika-tchika* of the crab scrambling along the rocky flats. There's the *squish-squish* of the clam squirting water as he burrows into the low tide sands. There's the *plop* of jumping trout and the *slap* of the salmon's tail clearing stream gravel to receive spawn. And in the forests you have the buzzing of insects, and the frogs croaking away, and the birds shrieking overhead. They were here a hundred million years ago."

It was only about ten thousand years ago that the first "natives" came over the now-submerged land bridge from Asia, which then spanned the Bering Straits. This coast offered them abundant hospitality.

Heavy rains created giant cedars from which the Indians could create their shelters, fashion their canoes, and carve their totem poles. Fullsome streams played host to salmon, endless kelp beds invited the herring's spawn. Without the need to migrate with their food supply, these people had time. With that time, and a unique sense of the natural world's oneness, they evolved rich and varied cultures along the entire coast.

Jutting out into the Pacific, the Queen Charlotte Islands are the place beyond; the farthest western shores. They have drawn to them a host of white settlers, of whom logger Dwayne Gould speaks.

"A lot of people who moved up here didn't like society as it was. They were a pioneering, independent type. They didn't ask anything of anybody, much like some of the young people today. The guy who wants to put a packsack on his back and just live along the beaches and enjoy the scenery – hell, that's the ideal life. The ones I really don't approve of are the ones who not only want to do that, but want benefits from the welfare office too. But the guy who just wants to really enjoy the country – maybe more of us should be doing it!"

Pacific in name only, the world's largest ocean constantly carves Canada's western shores. In time, the glaciated rocks about Pt. Renfrew will resemble the sands of Long Beach.

The ebbing waters of Barkley Sound reveal rich intertidal life. Flooding rivers bring forest ghosts to the shore.

The wonder of regeneration happens very quietly. A tiny calypso orchid gets pollinated by a mite, old trees fall and young ones seek the life-giving light.

Perched atop the rocks of Barkley Sound, cormorants and sea lions rest from Spring's hectic pace of courting and breeding.

Trumpeter swans arrive from the Arctic to winter on Alberni Inlet. Elk leave snow-clad mountains to browse rainy valleys.

*Poised at Yaculta Rapids, an eagle scans turbulent waters — rises,
dives, and grasps a salmon in an ancient, deadly ballet.*

And man comes to these same waters, finds the salmon is to his liking, and begins to wonder how long this feast can go on.

They come from Alberta to quench their sea-longing, outwit a clam, seesaw on the sand and, somehow, find solitude together.

2
Our Own Land

"If the Canadian culture was based on its relationship to the land, we would have a very solid type of culture. But because they've avoided this thing, there is no definition that very clearly distinguishes Canadian culture from anything else."

The words of Phillip Paul express the sentiments of many British Columbia Indians appraising their relationship with the white man's world. They're willing to work with it, but they want a personal way that is their own. Once they had one, and they thrived alongside a coastline of abundance. Sea and forest responded bountifully to their foraging efforts. But the "coming of the white man" to North America set off a chain of events that left native people with a confused sense of identity.

Fully one-third of Canada's native population lived in what was to become the Province of British Columbia. The North Coast population has been divided by modern ethnographers into seven language groups. Moving down the coast they are Tlingit (their land lies in Alaska's Panhandle), Haida, Tsimshian, Kwakiutl, Nootka, Bella Coola and Coast Salish. These people were further divided into bands, each with a chief holding the land in the name of his people. Advised by his counsellors, aware of his traditions, concerned with the limitations of the land, the leader attempted to conserve wisely the natural resources at hand.

In many localities, the cultural resources have dwindled. When the Haida from Masset raised their first totem pole in eighty years, they could not celebrate with dance. Their own dances had been forgotten. Tsimshian dancers from the mainland had to come to the Queen Charlottes to aid in the ceremonies.

The young Haida are trying to go back, trying to get to their roots. Alfie Collinson is one Haida from Skidegate who went searching. His livelihood comes from fishing salmon, and carving argilite totem poles. His two-storey home would look in place on a New Westminster street, but his heart would feel out of place there. Alfie knows he belongs in the Queen Charlottes. It was Alfie's kinsmen who greeted British Columbia's first explorer, the Spaniard Juan Perez, as he sailed out of the fog in July of 1774. Within a hundred years, the white man's society would be established; by the turn of this century, the Indians' longhouses would be abandoned. Alfie and a friend recently cruised the islands, visiting the villages of long ago, to sense and record their heritage.

"One village that I went into, I felt like I just fell back in time . . . a hundred, two hundred years ago . . . went into one house . . . just the long beams and the house pit were there. When I was sitting in that pit, there was a beehive on a tree close by, and you could hear them humming away . . . all talking together . . . and there was a bird on the tree there whistling, sounded like someone whistling a tune, like a person walking and whistling a tune . . . and I was just gone when I was there. Dug around and found a coin, a big Chinese coin with a hole in the middle."

There is no mystery about how the Chinese coin got to Tanu. For the first seventy-five years of their presence on the sea charts of the civilized world, Canada's western shores were a prime destination for merchant vessels involved in the fur trade with China. It was Captain James Cook who really "discovered" this world. Searching for a North American sea lane from Europe to Asia, he visited what we now know as Friendly Cove on Vancouver Island's Nootka Sound.

No one had a better sense of the white man's impact than Captain Cook. As he left Tahiti for the northern latitudes on his last voyage, he wrote:

"I cannot avoid expressing it as my real opinion that it would have been far better for these poor people never to have known our superiority in the accommodations and arts that make life comfortable . . . they cannot be restored to that happy mediocrity in which they lived before we discovered them. . . . For, by the time that the iron tools, of which they are now possessed, are worn out, they will have almost lost the knowledge of their own. A stone hatchet is, at present, as rare a thing amongst them as an iron one was eight years ago, and a chisel of bone or stone is not to be seen."

The English merchant-adventurer John Meares, trading under a Portuguese flag of convenience with Chief Wicananish, noted in June of 1788: "Sea otter skins and other furs were now produced to the number of thirty, and of the most beautiful kind; which after a considerable deal of negotiation we at length purchased; for we found to our cost, that these people, like those of Nootka, possessed all the cunning necessary to the gains of mercantile life."

Meares was aware of other elements of their behaviour: "Gratitude is a virtue well known on this distant shore." He characterized a Nootka noble, Callicum, as "possessed of a delicacy of mind and conduct which would have done honour to the most improved state of our civilization." The gift offerings which flowed between chiefs as they met and feasted impressed him greatly. Meares ingratiated himself with Chief Maquinna, and claimed to have gained special rights for trading, land purchase, and the erection of an outpost at Nootka Sound.

Here history enters the incredibly foggy passage known as the Nootka Sound Incident. Round One was fought at Nootka Sound itself. The Spaniards, fearful of foreign encroachments on shores they considered theirs by right of discovery, sailed north from California, halted all English trading activity, built a fort and settled in. Round Two was fought in Europe, where George III's Prime Minister, Lord Pitt, forcefully contended that possession was dependent not on discovery but on occupation.

Round Three was never fought – readied for war, the English and Spanish fleets eyed each other in the channel as the Madrid Treaty of 1790 was signed.

Details of the settlement, which allowed England to implement the concessions made to Meares by Maquinna, were to be worked out at Nootka. Captain George Vancouver arrived there in August of 1792, commissioned to receive from the Spanish Commander, Juan Francisco de la Bodega y Quadra, those elements of land and structure which had been agreed upon by treaty. It soon became clear that what Meares had actually gotten from Maquinna was quite unclear. Vancouver and Quadra, unable to resolve matters, both sailed off. It was not until 1795 that the diplomats arrived at a solution, which was withdrawal of all parties from Nootka Sound itself. But England had established rights of trade and exploitation that it would in due time expand into control of Canada's western shores.

Captain Vancouver's log entry for September 6, 1792, provides unintended irony: "Maquinna and his two wives and some of his relatives returned our visit. They had not been long on board when I had great reason to consider my royal party as the most consumate beggars I had ever seen. . . . They demanded every thing which struck their fancy as being either useful, curious or ornamental. . . . I was, however, fortunate in having at hand everything requisite to satisfy the demands of Maquinna and his party." Did Vancouver ever consider, as had his former commander, James Cook, what he was about? Spain and England were essentially bargaining with each other for control over everything the Indian possessed.

These people were possessed of more than a remarkable land. Another English mariner, who lived with the Nootka for three years, noted: "These people are remarkably healthful and live to a very advanced age, having quite a youthful appearance for their years. They have scarcely any disease but the cholic. . . . During the whole time I was among them, but five natural deaths occurred . . . a circumstance not a little remarkable in a population of about fifteen hundred."

During the first seventy-five years of contact with Europeans, the coastal Indians enjoyed a period of seeming prosperity. Contact with whalers and fur traders provided trade goods for consumption and gifting at the increasingly larger potlatch feasts. But that same contact brought measles, influenza, tuberculosis, alcoholism, and venereal disease. By the 1860's, an estimated population of 80,000 in Cook's time had dwindled to 60,000. In 1862, a fleet of Haida canoes returned to the Queen Charlottes from Victoria with smallpox spreading amongst its paddlers. Three years later the ensuing epidemic subsided; native population had decreased by another 20,000. By 1929, the Indian population had shrunk to 22,000.

The most severely hit area was the Queen Charlottes; the Haida population shrank from 8,000 to 800. They have defied death and assimilation: now regaining their numbers, they are also regaining their heritage. At the Queen Charlotte City School, "Haida Studies 10" exposes native students to the importance of the sea and the cedar tree in Haida culture. One section is entitled "The Necessities of Life:" it explores the ancient methods of hunting and fishing and food preservation, the creation of clothing from fur animals and cedar bark, and methods of building the Haida Longhouse. Their teaching resources are diverse: films, tapes, native newspapers and magazines, books, and "resource people" – Haidas who have cherished their culture and, like Alfie Collinson, are building on it. But the biggest resources of all are the students.

They live in the environment of their ancestors and the environment of modern Canada. And they are wondering how both will survive. Aware of what's happening to the ecology, they know that a landscape is scarred when oil drillers leave behind dry holes and empty oil drums; they know that seals and shell-fish are killed when a tanker leaks its load. In their eyes, the forest around them is being turned into a stumpyard. Asked the importance of the land, they have answers that are uniquely theirs.

"Our ancestors lived off the land before the white men came around. They were living pretty good. They had no complaints. There was no smallpox. We all lived in harmony with nature – it isn't the idea of conquering nature, it's the idea of living with it. You don't try to subdue it. You don't make the rain fall when you want it to, you don't make the deer come to you when you want them to – you're supposed to live with them. When the deer come, you hunt them; when the rain falls, you build yourself a shelter. You can't control nature; it's something that has to control you. The white man has to control everything – if it doesn't listen to you, you just wipe it right out. We love the land – we don't want to get away from it. The kids that go out to Prince Rupert and Vancouver to school, they all come back – they don't like the city. They come back and take correspondence courses."

Some Indians, like Karen Johnson, have tried to make their way in the white man's world. Licensed as a practical nurse, this Tsimshian girl has worked in Victoria's hospitals. When she speaks of her youth along the Nass River, her dark eyes glow, her smile brightens your life. You listen as she tells of one of the great runs of oolachen, a tiny fish so rich in oil the white man calls it "candlefish." Her voice's melody lends enchantment to the story it imparts.

"There was a lot of dancing, a lot of feasting – it was a really happy time. It lasted for about four days. My dad was handing down his grease-making techniques to his granchildren, so it was quite a big thing. It's really busy – seems like all the people on the reserve are one big family – well, they are all year round, but particularly at that time, and at salmon time too. All the women are together then, helping with smoking and salting. They feed the men all at one time. It's just one big thing; it's *really* nice. The oolachen run has a happy sound. Each time someone brings in a brail full of oolachens, everybody's shouting and laughing and having a good time. Our oolachen spot is about thirty-five miles away from the reserve. Just before the season starts, the men go down, gather up fire wood, build a campsite – they have to live there for about a month. The oolachen are full of grease, and you use that grease for cooking, and you eat it, just like a dip. But it's more than just grease; it's a part of our lives. It's part of being happy."

Recently returned to work on his reserve, Ron Hamilton is Opetchesaht – one of the thirteen bands collectively called Nootka by anthropologists. His ancestors on Vancouver Island were amongst the first to trade with the white man. He is twenty-six years old. His head bears a mane that falls past his shoulders, and a wisdom that goes beyond his years. Ron's an artist with wood, silver, pen, and ink. He works with the West Coast District Council of Indian Chiefs in Port Alberni, putting his head at the service of natives who want to learn more about their cultural heritage. Ron has prepared a group of drawings for the District's paper – *Ha-Shith-Sa (Interesting News)*. In pre-contact times, the coastal people were all dependent on the forest and the sea. Their houses, food, vessels, ceremonial masks, and totem poles were richly decorated with figures that came out of their environment. A handful of traditional forms were used all along the coast to represent fish scales, whale fins, raven eyes. Much like a music professor explaining the notes and chords from which a song can be composed, Ron was presenting the various forms used in North Coast art.

"The way designs were constructed was a tradition, but the actual designs themselves weren't. Every artist had his own taste, his own way of doing things, his own place for colours. But the figures – the killer whale, the wolf, the thunderbird, the eagle, the raven – those things were all traditional to our art. It's pretty highly structured – a sea-serpent has to look like a sea-serpent, not a wolf – but the way you draw them is up to you. It's like flamenco guitar music. There's bits and pieces that they use to construct a melody, and when you hear flamenco guitar, you know you are listening to flamenco guitar. You don't think that's country-western. Flamenco guitar is played within set, familiar boundaries, and yet two different flamenco guitarists will play the same piece quite differently."

Ron feels that the best way his people found to conserve resources and make sure they yielded from year to year was to be reasonable about their use. He tells a story about a spring salmon run:

"Three young boys – I don't know what the hell got in their heads – got an idea that they could shoot arrows in the back of the spring salmon and put fire on those arrows. Then they could watch the fire go up the river. That's just stupid, a meaningless thing to do; but they did it. And in the story, the whole world, the whole world that these people knew, which, of course, was just their own village – they didn't travel all over the place, they lived in their own village, they knew that land intimately, they didn't have to go anywhere else, their food was there, their recreation areas were there, everything they needed was in their own area – but this whole world of theirs caught on fire. That was due to these kids playing with those arrows, shooting them in the backs of fish. That may never have happened, but it's a story that illustrates a belief. You don't mess around with something that's valuable to you. If you want the spring salmon to come to you, to feed your people, you mind that thing, you don't waste it."

The most familiar North Coast art form is the Totem Pole, a family history in three dimensions. Its animal forms represent crests the family has a right to use. Describing the Totem Pole's function, Ron launched into a description of the social world from which they spring.

"There are dances and songs connected with totem pole figures; they might represent spiritual connections or supernatural happenings. A man might have been spoken to by a grizzly bear and his son would carve one on their family pole to represent that. Or the pole could have crests that were given to the family by other tribes. Let's say I marry a woman from Alaska. She's Tlingit. Her family owns a halibut crest, and when I marry her, they pass on to my children the right to use that halibut crest. Now when my son is thirty years old, he might say to visitors: 'My crest is the halibut, I can carve on a pole woman holding a sea otter, woman holding a spring salmon, two wolves from my father and mother's side.' And somebody would say, 'No, you don't own that – who said you own that? I don't think you own that.'

"There's no way to claim it publicly unless he turns around and he puts up a potlatch, a big feast, and he claims these things and he has people speak from different areas. Chief of Kyuquot stands up and says: 'This boy's great-great-grandfather came from Kyuquot, that man's father was the second chief of Kyuquot. The songs that he owns are these – Hamitsa – he'll name those things, tell those people. You people, Opetchesaht, this boy that's one of you, his songs come from here, these are his,' and they give it to my son again. They publicly do it again. Each generation has to stand up and claim in their own time what is theirs. It's not my responsibility to stand up and look after the next generation; they have to stand up and look after themselves. But where you can help, you help.

"You stand up and you share your wealth, you feed people, you entertain people, you give people presents, you pay people – you pay them money – *potl-payaa* – you pay people to witness something that's going to happen. And it's a transfer of a name from me to my son.

"The first name that I was given was Hupquatchew. You receive five – six – ten names in your life-time. You've got a baby name, you've got a young man's name, you've got a name from both sides of your family, you've got a name given to you when you do something special, you've got a potlatch name. One of my potlatch names is Kwaweena.

"There was a law against potlatching for eighty years. It was really a law against taking part in our culture, because the potlatch was its core. The potlatch was a religious thing, an economic thing, a legal thing. People were paid to do things publicly, debts were paid publicly. You get six hundred – a thousand people together for four days; you've got to think that's a social event. It was everything. A chance to communicate, people from different villages came – they said: 'Ah boy, you know the wild crabapples up in Kyuquot are just ripe right now.' Another says: 'You should see the river in Nanaimo, dog salmon by the millions – too much, too much dog salmon. Do you need dog salmon?' And I say: 'Isn't that something – we got no dog salmon this year, but we got lots of berries – do you want to trade?' There's a chance for commerce to take place. There's a chance for political things to happen. People stood up and said: 'This is my position, these fishing rights have been passed on to me, this is what I own – does anybody disagree with that. This is what I'm passing on to my children.' There was dance, there was song, all those things – and for eighty years it was against the law to do them. In the 1920's they really cracked down – they took much of the ceremonial gear: masks, rattles, blankets, bowls, whistles, off to Ottawa. The Anti-Potlatch Law was lifted in 1952. Now they say: 'Well, when you build a museum to house it, we'll give it back.' That's nonsense. To an Indian, a mask doesn't belong in a museum; it belongs on a face, on a date, in a certain time, in a certain place, in a

certain song. *Now* it's saying something. It doesn't mean anything in a glass case staring out at you."

Anthropologists have witnessed potlatches ad infinitum. Theories as to their origin and function are varied. Some saw it as an Indian war with money, others as conspicuous consumption gone wild, still others as a good, functional way to establish and preserve the social fabric. But all agree on one thing – the word potlatch is found in the chinook trade jargon and it means "to give". Why was the potlatch outlawed? One anthropologist offers this explanation: "Certain natives had made so much money, using the European economy to their own ends. They really irked the missionaries and Indian agents. They saw them go out, make the money and then, of all things, give the money away. What blasphemy!"

Many young anthropologists see themselves as suppliers of a service to the Indian people. Some are aiding Indians in land claims research. They have seen museums evolve a new policy – when a ceremonial object is purchased from a family today, an agreement is made to keep the object available for ceremonial functions. The anthropologists themselves bring it to the function. Far from being academic empire-builders, they hope that in ten years these services will be rendered by locally-run Indian museums. By that time, anthropologists' functions as modern court reporters with camera and tape recorder at potlatches will have been taken over by the Indians. One anthropologist is acutely aware of a personal yield from his work in British Columbia: "I've gained the sense of a world view that grew out of this environment – the culture that you and I carry with us did not grow here."

The European culture of which he speaks got its permanent footing on the North Coast when British fur traders were squeezed north from the Oregon country by expansionist Yankees. The Hudson's Bay proprietary colony of Vancouver Island was founded in 1849; the mainland colony of British Columbia came into being pursuant to the gold rush of 1858. Consolidated in 1866 as the Crown Colony of British Columbia, it confederated with the Dominion of Canada as the Province of British Columbia in 1871.

Indians up and down the coast felt as did the Tsimshian tribal leaders along the Nass River in 1877: "What we don't like about the Government is their saying this: 'We will give you this much land.' How can they give it when it is our own? They have never bought it from us or our forefathers. They have never fought and conquered our people and taken the land that way, and yet they say now that they will give us so much land – our own land."

A footnote in Wilson Duff's *Indian History of British Columbia* offers partial answer to the Indian's quandary: "It is important not to confuse Indian title with the absolute or underlying title to the land. Absolute title (a European concept) has been vested in the Crown ever since Britain, Spain, Russia, and the United States, without consulting any Indians, settled the questions of sovereignty over this continent. The Indians of Canada, whether by choice or not and whether they have treaties or not, are subjects of the Crown, and the Crown owns the land. Of course the Indians did own the land previously under clearly defined concepts of ownership . . . by the Royal Proclamation and subsequent precedents the Crown has legally obligated itself to recognize and extinguish Indian title."

Along the British Columbia coast, the Crown has never confirmed its title by entering into treaties with the Indians. As Hudson's Bay Company Governor, James Douglas completed fourteen land treaties on the southern end of Vancouver Island between 1850 and 1852. As Crown Colony Governor, he established many reserves on an informal basis. His successors felt these reserves impeded settlement and were "in excess of the requirements of the aborigines." They deemed ten acres per Indian, rather than eighty, adequate for coastal conditions. In 1867, the Colonial Secretary disavowed the authority under which the treaties had been made. Appropriate authority was given, under the British North America Act, to the federal government to handle all relations with native people. But Crown title to the land of British Columbia rests with its provincial government. Whether unwilling or unable to finalize a treaty or satisfactory settlement for the last one hundred years, the coastal Indians have now banded together to fulfill their aspirations for an equitable settlement. For them, the existing reserves established by the federal government are inequitable. British Columbia's 189 bands now control 1620 reserves (there are 2241 in Canada) totaling 843,000 acres. If it seems like a lot, do a little arithmetic. The reserves average 520 acres apiece (consistent with their functions as fishing villages or seasonal foraging sites) and the 48,000 Indians of today have eighteen acres apiece of a 234,000,000-acre province.

One of these Indians, Danny Watts, was born on the Ahswinis Reserve of the Opetchesaht Band. Trained as a shipwright, Danny worked in Vancouver for many years. He is competently tackling the problems he faces as Executive Director for the West Coast District Council of Indian Chiefs. He watches over the day-to-day needs of thirteen bands and 3,500 people virtually non-dependent on the Bureau of Indian Affairs. Their self-government is novel.

"What started it all was just frustration. The Chairman of our District Council, George Watts, approached the Regional Office of Indian Affairs in Vancouver, and said, 'When are you guys going to start helping us out and try to give us some assistance instead of trying to hold us back? The lack of housing on reserves is becoming a very serious thing.' When they said, 'Why don't you do it yourself?', George Watts answered, 'What do you mean? You mean you'll give us the funding and let us handle it ourselves?' And they said, 'By all means.' So we discussed this and a couple of other programs such as education, and they said, 'If you think you're capable of doing it, go ahead and take that over too.' So George returned to the District Council, presented it to the chiefs and we tossed this idea around for a few months. Finally, George said, 'Let's not just sit around and talk about it – are we going to do it or aren't we?' And we said certainly, let's try it; so we approached the Regional Office in Vancouver and told them we wished to take over our own administration. They were very co-operative with us. If it wasn't for their co-operation I don't think we could have done it. They helped us in every way. Our funding and our sponsorship came out of the Regional Office in Vancouver, but Ottawa wasn't aware of it – in other words, they were sticking their necks out. But now Ottawa has recognized us as a responsibility centre, and we are more or less assuming the same responsibilities that the Department of Indian Affairs offices had in the past; but hopefully we're going to do a better job."

Danny makes a strong point that direction comes from his people at the band level, not from the top down. "Most of our workers are in the field, actually out in the field. It's not that they are dealing with problems alone – at Zabales there is an Indian logging outfit – a co-operative – a legitimate logging show with 360,000,000 cunits of wood alloted to them. They have enough wood for twelve years. Isolated Indian villages like Queens Cove will benefit directly from this activity.

"Dealing directly with the Department of Indian Affairs was very frustrating – it was just like a boy asking his parents, 'Can I do this; can I do that; can I have enough money to buy this?' And we couldn't make any decisions for ourselves. We couldn't say, 'This is what has happened on our reserve and this is what we're going to do.' We had to say, 'This is what's happening, can we do this?' And if they didn't like it, they'd say no. But now, we make the decision and we tell them what we want, which is the way it should be – they have a veto power; but they haven't used it. We've got some pretty capable people in the District Council; we don't make rash decisions; and if there is a possibility of a veto, we look at it very closely."

Estates and land transactions are still being handled by the Bureau. Danny feels that if the district makes a success of what it is doing today, Ottawa will say, "You guys are doing everything right now, why don't you take the whole thing." The District Council is currently responsible for education, social services, housing, capital projects, recreation, community development, economic development, a newspaper, and fishermen's assistance.

Six district bands have reserve lands within the park boundaries of the new Pacific Rim Park. Since 1969, the federal government has been negotiating to get the land. "We keep telling them – 'Go ahead, develop your parks the way you want them, but leave us alone.'" The Indians don't want money, they don't want to lease the land, they don't want to exchange it – even on a four acre for one basis. It's hard not to identify with them. The issue is rather simple – the people they invited in as guests are now trying to make

them sell the house. The Indian views the land he has left on this coast as his home. The white man wants to come there for the weekend. The Indian wants to continue living there forever.

In the Provincial Archives in Victoria there is a letter from Edward Banfield, an early settler, to James Douglas, then Her Majesty's Governor. In part, it reads: "My object of this time in talking about purchase of land was solely to prevent myself from native annoyance, Sir. An attempt by myself to make an example of honest dealing that they might perceive that white men would not occupy their valueless ground without purchase. They put no value on their land, as they do not cultivate."

Phillip Paul, a Saanich who directs land claims research for the Union of British Columbia Indian Chiefs has made a pointed and pungent response to Banfield's assumptions.

"He's a way off base. You know that 'land is valueless because of non-cultivation' is a complete misunderstanding; a misunderstanding that we've had historically with white society. Land is the whole spiritual essence of the Indian culture. It was *very* valuable. This is one of the reasons they were reluctant to cultivate. There didn't seem to be any object to doing this when the land had already provided everything they needed. Cultivation would be a violation of their understanding and relationship to the land. Indian people saw land as an extension of themselves rather than something that was quite separate. White settlement was allowed to happen here because of the fundamental concept of Indian culture – sharing. There was a lot of land, and obviously the people who arrived here didn't have any land. Our ancestors were willing to share it. Because the white society had a different concept of land, the Indian people got screwed."

In the years to come, jurists and legislators will be challenged by Indians claiming compensation for British Columbia's land and wealth. Whatever the results, there is already one verdict. Elizabeth George, 103 years of age, pronounced it at a West Coast District land claims meeting. She spoke of the people who envied the land so much: "They broke one of our basic laws – that you cannot steal!"

For generations sea-nurtured salmon have returned to spawn;
for generations the Kwakiutl have awaited them. Ways of
fishing change, but the salmon run is still the year's high point.

Races come to Chemainus Bay each spring. Eleven to a sleek canoe, they paddle as one. Although style in boats and clothing change, oneness with the water is a constant for Coastal Indians.

At races' end, the crews come together, warm themselves by the fire, feast on salmon, and speak of winter's passage.

A Kwakiutl chief's seat receives the last embellishment from its carver's hand. The community house at Alert Bay awaits the potlatch. Here they celebrate with dance, song, and sharing.

Inside the Kwakiutl community house, members of the family of a venerable elder perform their inherited dances. Presents are being prepared for guests at the potlatch honouring his late wife.

ANTHONY ISLAND PARK

THIS IS THE SITE OF THE ANCIENT HAIDA
INDIAN VILLAGE KNOWN AS NINSTINTS
ITS PEOPLE DECIMATED BY DISEASE & WAR
MOVED TO SKIDEGATE ABOUT 1890
THIS ISLAND HAS BEEN DESIGNATED A
PROVINCIAL PARK, AND ANY PERSON
WHO DAMAGES OR REMOVES ANY TOTEM POLE
OR OTHER RELIC IS PUNISHABLE BY LAW.

DEPT. OF RECREATION
AND CONSERVATION

61

In 1774, Captain Cook discovered a world strange to him. His artist Webber bartered brass uniform buttons for the right to sketch this view of the Nootka Sound longhouse.

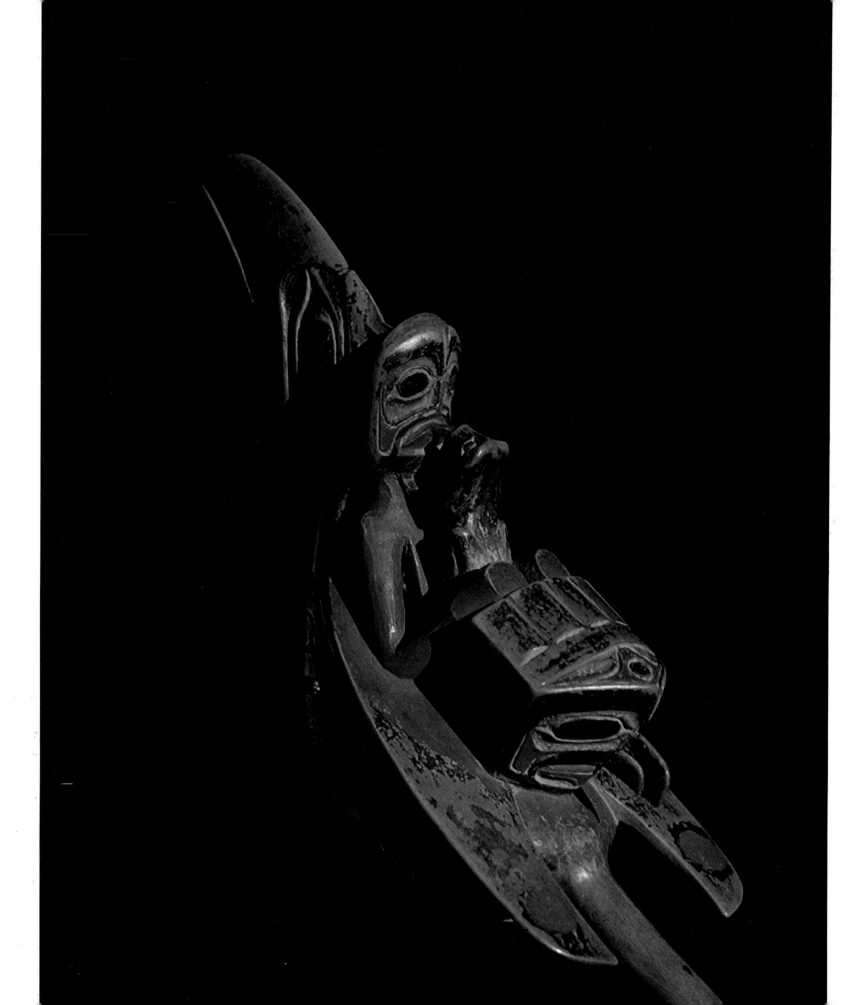

3

The Harvesting of a Growing Crop

"Come, ye children of enterprise and ambition –
all ye that are hungry and desolate, come and partake
of that which ye have long hoped and struggled for,
but never realized."

With gilded pen, Kinahan Cornwallis thus beckoned his fellow Englishmen to join the gold rush of 1858 and depart for that land described in his book *The New Eldorado – British Columbia.* And come they did, "to gather gold and plant intelligence in the newly awakened wilderness." The glittering gravel bars of the Fraser River had already attracted hordes from California by the time England established the mainland colony of British Columbia on November 19, 1858. Determined to maintain effective sovereignity above the forty-ninth parallel, London dispatched a detachment of Royal Engineers to aid James Douglas, now Governor of both northwest colonies. They were to build roads and restrain the 25,000 goldseekers who arrived mostly from California by year's end.

Victoria was transformed from an orderly outpost of the Hudson's Bay Company's fur empire into a bustling gold camp. Cast-iron buildings sprang up on Front Street, ships disgorged English, Chinese, and Australians. Sacks of gold poured out of new strikes in the mainland's interior. Dazzling prospects were sensed on all sides.

After the Dominion of Canada was born in 1867, British Columbia (united by merger of the two colonies in 1866) pondered, "Whither goest we – to Union with America or confederation with Canada." To the north was America's Alaska Territory (acquired from the Tsar in 1867), to the south were America's Washington Territories. The prospect of confederation with Canada, centred politically and economically in the distant east, dismayed many whose fortunes had fallen with the passage of the gold-rush days. A hundred Victoria residents, many of whom had San Francisco business connections, signed a petition of annexation to President Ulysses S. Grant. They expressed concern that ". . . this Colony is now suffering great depression, owing to its isolation, a scarcity of population and other causes too numerous to mention."

The Loyalist backlash to this petition aided the supporters of confederation. On March 9, 1870, Attorney General Henry Crease addressed his colleagues in the Legislative Council: "May He who holds the fate of Nations in the hollow of His hand, and crowns with success, or brings to naught, the counsels of men, guide all our deliberations to such an issue as shall promote the peace, honour and welfare of our Most Gracious Sovereign and of this and all other portions of Her extended realm."

The council sent a delegation east – gallingly, they had to use a route through the United States – to negotiate the terms of confederation. When in 1871 Ottawa agreed to build an all-Canadian transcontinental railroad and to assume the Colony's $1,045,000 debt, the Crown Colony voted to become the Province of British Columbia. Soon she was Canada's portal on the Pacific. Logging camps were filled by miners who hadn't found their claims. From British Columbia's docks, sailing ships carried more and more lumber and salmon to world markets. The harvest of the coast was under way.

There were few open lands where crops could be raised and cattle could forage. The landscape was really just mountains and trees, and more mountains and more trees. Centuries of one hundred inches of rain a year had created coastal forest the European could barely comprehend.

Two men had to saw through the day to bring down one 200-foot fir. Within decades, lumbermen had brought in giant steamyarders and portable railroads to aid their efforts.

For some, the forest was an enemy to be got rid of, so they could get on with the farming. As one flies along the coast today, their clearings, gone back to the wild, stand out. The would-be farmers who tried to tame the land and lost went off and built fishing boats. They swore at the stubborn forest even as they hauled their laden halibut lines and salmon nets. But these waters could really provide.

Virgin forests, unfished seas, unmined mountains: the climax of eons of creation. It took nearly a century for anyone to see clearly that there was a limit; that you had to sow where you had reaped.

"In the old days, we went out halibut fishing and did a job. Set out twenty-eight skates of long line, 300 fathoms to a skate, five days a week – now the boats are tied up four to five days a week. I think we did fish it out." Webb Pierce has borne a brisk Nova Scotia twang into his retirement years. He came west because "there were only a few guys back in Nova Scotia that had all the money – and they wanted you to work for nothing. Some of the richest men in B.C. today are the fishermen."

Webb worked the water world out of Prince Rupert. He was slammed about on halibut boats in Hecate Straits, fished round the clock during the Nass and Skeena salmon runs. He worked in the canneries and ran packer boats to them from the fishing fleet. After a year on the beach, during which he really got to know his nine grandchildren and spent the first summer in thirty-nine with his wife at their lake cabin, the itch was in him. "Keep telling my wife I'm going to get me a job. I think next year I'll go back-packing – to meet the boys again. Next summer, I'll just go out on the sockeye season."

Ken Harley's accent is pure Bristol. British Merchant Marine in World War II, then fishing in the Queen Charlottes till fifteen years ago. Now he's skipper of the *Sooke Post*, patrol vessel for the Fisheries Service of the Department of the Environment. Biologists determine how best to manage the stocks, by establishing closed areas or closed days. Ken and his crew keep things straight thereafter.

"When I fished commercially years ago, people used to go inside the boundaries and steal fish – no one used to think much about it. They thought they were just taking it from the fisheries department. But there are not too many dishonest fishermen left on the coast. Now, they hate to see another fisherman go across the boundary of a closed area. They know if he takes halibut out, there'll be fewer that work their way across the boundary for them to catch. It'll come eventually that they will help police it themselves. They'll have to if they want to get their share of the fish."

Fishermen have seen salmon runs decline. But they realized their own overfishing was not the only villain. Industrial and urban pollution, as well as logging, had disrupted many spawning grounds. But the runs are increasing now. Federal and provincial authorities are clamping down on the polluters, and the Fisheries Service has begun to learn how to manage the river systems to maximize salmon yield. By monitoring fish that were finclipped as sea-bound fry, biologists learn the destination of each new wave of returning migrants. Closures are established to assure adequate fish escapement for spawning. Computer models which take into account water conditions throughout the route "home" are now being developed by the Fisheries Service.

Salmon returning to the Fulton River, a tributary of the Skeena, numbered 2,400,000 in 1974; up from 500,000 in 1964. This miracle was accomplished by the installation of artificial spawning grounds, which accommodated 260,000 spawning salmon. More than 1,500,000 fish found their way into fishermen's nets. Other streams which are capable of nurturing more fry, but which have inadequate spawning areas, have been spotted along the rivers that run down to the Pacific. One under development is the Capilano, which empties right into Vancouver's harbour. Its salmon run has become a stellar tourist attraction.

British Columbia is managing to keep its stocks of fish up to a level that is probably the envy of a lot of other coastal nations. They are working hard to maintain this resource against quite high odds. As one fisheries biologist realizes:

"With all the complex technological changes that have been occurring, we have to be able to keep control of this resource; or we'll lose it all."

The major resource of the B.C. coast is forest – stands of Douglas, Fir, Hemlock, Cedar. Most of the mature timber that is being cut today is three hundred to a thousand years old. The forest industry lets no one forget that it is the biggest employer and revenue producer in the province. But it is not the biggest landholder. Ninety-five percent of the province's surface is in Crown name, administered by the province for the public good. And the forest industry is no longer in charge of defining the public good. As Secretary of State for the Colonies in 1858, Edward George Lytton made sure that the Crown retained land ownership in British Columbia. Specific resources, not the land itself, were to be leased for development. As a result of the ecological clamour of the last decade, a major re-evaluation of resource use got underway. One of the first challenges was to understand how the forest ecosystem works, and how man affects it.

Dawn at the mouth of the Sarita River – gull shrieks, raven calls, waves on the shore, rain in the forest, a "crummy" load of fallers outbound with their chainsaws, trees crashing to the forest floor, whistle signals to the yarder, whining grinding log-laden trucks setting out for Port Alberni's mills. Dawn at the mouth of Carnation Creek, one mile away on Vancouver Island's Barkley Sound – gulls, ravens, waves, rain – and a silence that will last five years.

For five years, Federal Fisheries is studying every element in the Carnation watershed's untouched ecosystem – something that has never been known before. Then the trees will fall before the chainsaw. Another five years will pass, and the stripped forest's recovery will be studied as closely as was its maturity. Then they will know more about coastal forests, and how to maintain them for maximum fish protection and the public good.

Presently, most of the coastal forest is under a twenty-one-year tree-farm licence to major lumber and pulp producers. It is their responsibility to manage, with the advice and consent of the Provincial Forestry Service, the timber resource. Better genetic stock, optimum spacing and thinning, efficient fertilization, and ecologically sound logging methods are all being developed. Their goal is an efficient forest that will yield a cut of marketable timber every seventy years.

Bob MacMillen runs the Port Renfrew Tree Farm for British Columbia Forest Products. His goal is to get the timber out efficiently. A tall man, with years of woods experience behind him, a straight talker, he looks you right in the eye. "No matter how you slice it, a logged-over area looks pretty messy. We helped an Indian carver a while back to get out some big cedar for totem poles. Came into a spot where we'd been burning slash the year before. He said one word, 'Hiroshima.' But bring a forester out there and right off he'd spot the two-year-old trees we'd just planted. Take a wheat field. It looks like hell after harvest, but the bread tastes good. What people see they interpret as destruction – but it's really the harvesting of a growing crop."

Each morning Bob's crews fan out across the southwest coast of Vancouver Island. They're a rugged lot with names all their own – the Bull Buck Boss has charge of the tree fallers, the Bull Cook watches after the bunkhouse, and there's the whistle punk, the boom-men, and the timber cruiser. Listen in at the squawk box in a pickup:

"Al said the ripper tooth on that dozer blade is gone."

"Just keep going – we'll have a new one out to you this afternoon."

"What's happening on Pandora Main Line?"

"There's a 'Cat' and a drill in there."

They're getting ready to blast rock; building road, pushing into another valley. The loggers need access to new loading sites.

Pushed by the public for recreational access, the tree farms have opened these logging roads to the back country. Many pressure groups have views about forest use that are at variance with those held by the loggers of the "cut and get out" era. Bob Franson, Professor of Law at the University of British Columbia, is actively involved in the Sierra Club's conservation efforts. He was one of many in both the public and industrial camps who felt frustrated in their efforts to resolve conflicts over how forests should be utilized and protected. "Since it was the government's responsibility to manage the resource, we realized that consensus had to be arrived at in a context in which government was present and participating, rather than caught "between."

That context now exists as the Public Liaison Committee, meeting quarterly in Vancouver under the auspices of the Council of Forest Industries. Its roster of delegates is indicative of how many interests are at stake. Federation of Mountain Clubs, Steelhead Society, Sierra Club, Pacific Salmon Society, Federation of Naturalists, Wildlife Federation, and The Environmental Council come from the public interest sector. The province's Forest Service, Fish and Wildlife Branch, Parks Branch, and the Federal Fisheries Service represent government. The Council of Forest Industries delegation includes representatives from forestry, logging, pulp and lumber, and ecological research. This forum is a unique means of cutting through both red tape and rancour on many topics of common interest.

"Dialogue is the name of the game," says Bill Young, Assistant Chief Forester in the British Columbia Forest Service. "The first meeting everybody started out with very strong positions. The Steelhead Society saying to protect the fish, 'there must be an inviolate sixty-six-foot green strip on either side of every stream – regardless.' Industry saying, 'we can't have that.' Nothing would work. Now we've reached a consensus involving site-specific considerations. In some places a sixty-six-foot strip isn't necessary, in other places it is desirable, in still others it's insufficient, and in some places we simply have to defer cutting. They say that confrontation is a good way of pinpointing the problem; but it's a deadly way of trying to resolve it."

They have agreed to hold their meetings without the presence of the press. This in itself is a giant step forward from the publicity battles that accompanied the dawn of ecological consciousness. They are reaching out to establish areas of agreement, rather than erect barriers of blame.

Grant Ainscough, Chief Forester for Macmillan-Bloedel, Ltd., sits as Chairman of the Liaison Committee. "We've all changed our stands. Any time you get people moving towards you, you can afford to move towards them."

The forester can renew his resource. The miner consumes his permanently. Ore bodies cannot be replaced. The Coastal Mountains are dotted with abandoned mining towns, ghostly witnesses to "fully developed properties."

Stewart is one place that refused to die. Tucked behind Alaska at the head of Portland Canal, on the northernmost stretch of the B.C. shore, the town is now going through a second boom phase. Ian MacLeod was born there. His father worked at the now-closed Premier Gold Mine, and he worked on the development phase of the Grand Duc Copper Mine. As hotel owner and mayor, he is concerned about Stewart's future. And he knows its past.

"The Premier Mine earned 130 million between 1919 and 1956, and yet you can look around Stewart and you won't see one thing it left behind – not one hospital, not one school, not one park. All the profits, all the tax money went south. At first, the profits were going to American owners, then they went to English owners. Victoria and Ottawa got the tax money. In recent years, the Grand Duc Mine has become our mainstay. It pays a terrific amount of local taxes. As a result, we've got first class schooling, an ice arena, a swimming pool. We have a water and sewer system, a sewage treatment plant. All of this is due to taxation on the company that is exploiting the ore body. A lot of money is staying within the community. That's the difference between the old and the new. Political evolution is really responsible. There's been a lot of pressure from the local level, and a lot more understanding from corporate citizens and members of Parliament and the B.C. Legislative Assembly."

In the old days, Stewart was not allowed to extend its township limits to include the Premier campsite, fifteen miles away. Available tax money could only build a grade school. Today the township extends more than thirty miles away, and that's how long the road is to the Grand Duc Mine site. One-third of the miners live in Stewart with their families. While the kids go to a modern high school, their fathers bus it up a mountain pass protected from avalanches by cannon-firing road crews. The men then pile onto the man-haul train for the ten-mile trip, part of it beneath of glacier, to work the ore body.

Ralph Mattson is the mine boss. He's worked copper for twenty years, all over North and South America. "I came here to make money, just like anybody else. The problem with mining is you've got such a tremendous investment. It's a helluva big gamble. Before you develop a property, your profit on paper has got to be damned attractive. Most companies want to get their money back in five to ten years. If they can't get that money back in twenty years, they're not going to fool with it, because the copper prices go up and down and new materials come on the market to compete with it. The critics think that miners are just tycoons, making a tremendous profit and they're abusing the resource. But for every mine that makes it, there are ten that don't."

Many people come to this coast to make a stake and leave. Some, like Hap Kearns, stay and "plant intelligence in the wilderness." "I couldn't live in Vancouver where you just move in and everything is laid on for you. I'd rather be the guy who's building the advancements. Every day you have challenges come up – that's when you've got to find a new route to get the job done." Hap's scrapbook has an underground portrait of his crew putting in the catenary system for Grand Duc's ten-mile tunnel. And there are shots of Hap working up the foundations for Stewart's sewage plant and Hap topping off the roof of the swimming pool. And if Ian MacLeod has his way, those facilities will be used long after Grand Duc shuts down. Plans are being made to expand logging operations out of Stewart, with a municipally owned lumber mill on the receiving end. That will give the community of Stewart the future that it is seeking.

Most people who work along the coast fly in and out of Prince Rupert aboard a Grumman Goose flown by Trans-Provincial Airlines. The company's routes span some of the world's most beautiful fjords. A look out the window on take-off from Prince Rupert provides a glimpse of man's transportation problems on this coast. Below are the railroad and highway which lead to Prince George. No rail or road system heads down-coast. The bus to Vancouver moves through the Okanagan Valley and passes along the Fraser River Canyon before arriving at the flat, densely occupied lower mainland. Pilot Larry Veech flies to Stewart regularly. "Awesome" and "fantastic" are words he uses to describe the scenery; "tough" is the word he uses to describe flying along the coast. His biggest concern is the weather.

"Prince Rupert is situated between the Portland Canal on the north and the Skeena River on the south. In the winter, you always have cold air from the interior coming down the valleys. We sit between the valleys and we're right on the coast. In comes a warm southeast front and everything dumps on us. In the summer, you can have blue skies all around, but within a twenty-mile radius of Prince Rupert the flying weather will be marginal. I pick the biggest, darkest cloud and fly under it and I'm home."

The three industries – forestry, fishing, and mining – that dominate the coast's economic life have developed their own special image. Ever-increasing size is the hallmark of all of them. In the early days of logging, touring photographers delighted in posing the woodsmen on the slim springboards that supported their labours just above the tree's swollen butt, axes shining and jagged bucksaws at the ready.

Today, the scale has changed. The forest is smaller than man. One-man chain saws do what was once a full day's work in thirty minutes. Machinery that can lift ten tons of logs like a bundle of matchsticks is commonplace. Giant off-highway trucks have replaced oxen, diesel power has replaced steam. The harvest efficiency which allows B.C. to compete in world markets is epitomized by the self-dumping log barges. The barges' own cranes perform the task of loading the timber at the Queen Charlotte Islands. Towed to the mills which ring the Straits of Georgia, these towering devices deliver their load of 20,000 tons by harnessing the sea. Slowly, the ballast tanks on one side of the barge are filled; the load tilts, creaks, and slides off into the water. A giant wave is launched as a forest is delivered.

The old loggers know better than the new ones how times have changed. They've gone through more. One blunt boss sees it this way: "In the long run, we're all dead. We have to see what our children's requirements will be. We have to adjust our use of the resource base to a level that can be perpetuated, and we can't wait until we're pushed into it. Human beings seem to react very well once they've been kicked in the pants, but until that time, they don't seem to react very well at all. Industry today has to operate in the context of an acceptable social philosophy. Those who adapt, survive. Those who don't, go under. There are a lot of logging companies on this coast which have gone out of existence simply because they couldn't adapt to the new realities. The right to manage the resource, which is what we get when the province issues a twenty-one-year tree-farm license, brings increasing responsibility to the public along with it."

One ecologist, who has been thinking hard about the province's future, sums up the feelings of many concerned people: "We have limitations on fishing, we have limitations on timber development, we have restrictions on mining. Whether they are adequate enough to sustain and protect our resources in the long run is a very difficult question. The thing we don't understand is what the long-term effect of massive human development on this coast will be. Personally, I hope that British Columbians realize what they've got and that they reflect on this once in a while and do something to perpetuate it. It's very difficult after something has disappeared to visualize what it was like before. This coast is tremendously rich and varied, unique as far as Canada is concerned. I think it's a pretty special place."

By creating additional spawning grounds, where fry can prosper in predator-free waters, biologists have more than quadrupled the run of Fulton River salmon.

Prince Rupert's waterfront is alive with tourist steamers and fishing boats. Halibut and cod are processed into frozen fillets by the thousands and shipped off to feed a fish-hungry world.

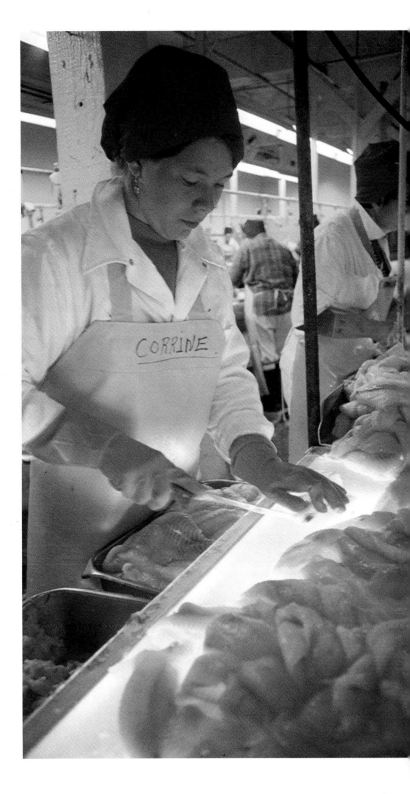

In the fifty miles this ferry steams through the Grenville Channel, its passengers will view only uninhabited shores.

Since man is nature's only challenger, he has had to learn to sow where he has reaped. But giants like these shall never be seen in the forest again, unless that forest is called a park.

Big machines, big companies. They call it the forest products industry. It fills half of the lunchboxes in British Columbia.

"People out here are more nice, more normal – you simply have to get along in a place like this."

His railroad will take copper concentrate to a waiting Japanese
ship. The lumber is bound for Britain, the aluminum for Toronto.

Quebec is his home – Grand Duc is his challenge. The mine camp gets 110 feet of snow a year; its shaft goes under a glacier.

The gold has run out at Premier, the people have gone and the snow has won. Ore can't be renewed like a fishery or a forest.

In small places up and down the coast they live the quiet moments of which the good life is made.

4

A Beacon in the Night

"The low, fertile shores we had been accustomed to see, though lately with some interruption, here no longer existed; their place was now occupied by the base of the stupendous snowy barrier, thickly wooded, and rising from the sea abruptly to the clouds; from whose frigid summit, the dissolving snow in foaming torrents rushed down the sides and chasms of its rugged surface, exhibiting altogether a sublime, though gloomy spectacle."

Thus Captain George Vancouver, in April of 1792, described the area he was to name Howe Sound, immediately to the north of what is today the city of Vancouver and the surrounding Lower Mainland. The inland waterway on which he proceeded north provided sheltered waters but no shore inviting the white man's habitation. Later visitors perceived this primal forest to be unlike anything in the Old World. Thus it was no surprise that British Columbians crowded down to the bottom of the province, hugging the flat. They built no towns high on the coastal mountain plateau. And the small communities that were built along the coast came into being only to fill specific needs. Prince Rupert is the northern seat of the fishing industry. Kitimat's aluminum complex was built to tap the hydroelectric potential locked in the Coast range. Powell River devotes itself to converting the forest into pulp, paper, and lumber. But they are all at sea level, close to the water which links them to the outside world.

Although Alexander Mackenzie was to arrive in Bella Coola "from Canada, by land" in 1793, both discovery and settlement of the coast was accomplished from the sea. In 1843 Fort Victoria came into existence as an outpost of the Hudson's Bay Company fur empire. Indians from the whole coast brought their pelts here to trade. The log settlement evolved into the capital of the Hudson's Bay Company's proprietary colony, the capital of the Crown Colony of Vancouver Island, and finally the seat of government of British Columbia, both as Crown Colony and Canadian province. Through these passages it managed to develop a special quality that was not quite English, not quite Canadian, but very much Victorian.

Ladies who live in this city are hardly reticent about sharing their knowledge and their views. "We're named after the old queen. She was a special person. Look what she did for the British Empire. Women's Lib, if you like, has been going on ever since."

Born hard-by James Bay seventy years ago, Louise Iverson has seen much of the province as a teacher, migrating along with her miner husband. But in retirement, she returned to her native city and compiled a history of its James Bay community. The richest archive of all is her mind, and she shares it openly.

"Growing up in Victoria, it was very peaceful. We used to joke about the sidewalks being pulled in at nine o'clock at night. That wasn't true of course. But Victoria has had an atmosphere all its own. I remember Emily Carr, the artist. She was quite eccentric, just couldn't conform. Like so many other great people that just don't run in the groove. She always felt that animals were more friendly to her than human beings. I remember seeing her go to the corner store with the puppies in the carriage and the dogs trailing along behind."

Louise's scrapbooks overflow with faded photos of the old Victoria, much of which still lingers on. There are horse-drawn tallyho's passing along in 1910 between the Parliament Buildings and the Empress Hotel, ladies in long linen gowns and flowery bonnets sunning themselves in Beacon Hill Park, the Pacific Fleet of the British Navy at anchor in Esquimalt, a tea-party at the Lieutenant Governor's Mansion. Louise delights in the Provincial Museum's presentation of British Columbia as it was, and is.

"People come out spellbound, and they go back, because you can't take it all in on one visit. I remember coming upon the old railroad station from Port Moody inside the museum and I remember thinking, "How wonderful – people can see what the province looked like during its development. It all feels so alive. You can see an old mine, and there's an old cannery. They reveal the type of work that's helped build this province. You can see it and you can feel it."

There is another living museum in Victoria that merits attention. It is called The Empress Hotel. If one doesn't rent a room there one surely takes tea there. Each afternoon the grand piano keyboard in the lobby is gently played. And to its accompaniment, all of Victoria, real or imagined, seems present. In front of its massive windows, yachts of all sizes bob gently in the inner harbour. The deep blasts of the ferry *Coho's* docking horn reminds one that there is another nation just across Juan de Fuca's Straits – the United States.

The Empress lobby is full of demure tables upon which rest English china tea cups, the tiniest sandwiches and the richest cream cakes. It seems that the Empress will always be serving fruit salad to little girls who sit on the edge of their chairs listening to their parents' cultured conversation. They know not to run about, and they always return as adults to reassure themselves that nothing has changed.

But Victoria does change and grow – like all cities. Streets that witnessed lace-gowned colonial wives are now favoured with an abundance of pack-toting, denim-skirted, fiercely independent folk like "Big Annie." There's a laundromat up on Menzies Street where she fluffs up her sleeping bag when she's down-island visiting friends. In the winter, Annie has a way of finding jobs. Perhaps she'll wash dishes in Victoria or work at the pulp mill office up in Tahsis. But come summer she's out by Long Beach in the Pacific Rim National Park, and she thinks of it all winter. Thinks of the eagles watching her as she watches them, thinks of special tide pools that emerge when the moon comes full phase. And the trees and the clouds and the stars. And that summer up at Chesterman's beach when a lot of her friends had built houses out of driftwood and "the RCMP all jumped out of the bushes and they said: 'Put on your clothes and tear down your houses.' And everyone put on their clothes and tore down their houses and moved to the next beach. And a few days later they built the houses back up again and went back to Chesterman's. The RCMP decided to wait until the rain got 'em. It worked, they left in October."

Annie laughs and laughs at that, but she'd never want to go back to Chesterman's. "All those people come up with campers and line the beach like this far apart so they can't open their doors. And they've got it all wrecked. There's no driftwood left anymore. And it's a real drag."

But not all the young people who arrive in Victoria are heading out to the beach. Some, like Donna Chagnon, have come to stay. A community worker in James Bay, Donna delights in the city. "There are a lot of nice restaurants, unusual shops, and there are a lot of native crafts that I find interesting. But mostly, it's clean and it's pretty. There are a lot of beautiful things to see and there's a lot of greenness and lots of flowers in the summertime. And go just one mile outside of Victoria and you're into the wild countryside. And the fact that it's a retirement centre helps to keep the city mellow. You see the seniors out walking on Dallas Road right in the middle of the winter, and they couldn't do that on the prairies. They all look so healthy. I enjoy elderly people, they're just tremendous, really neat. They love to be around young people. And they're really loving. Even though they hardly know you, they'll call you "dear" and they'll put their arms around you, and they just make you feel very good. They've lived an awful long time, and some of them have done such fascinating things, it's just incredible.

"Met one woman who, as a young girl, discovered the first emerald mine in Norway. Then she prospected all around the central and northern parts of Ontario, filing claims for an English mining company. She camped out, spent her whole early years surrounded by men, eventually married a guy who became an Indian agent. So she went out and finagled for some sewing machines and she taught the Indian women how to sew and cook. Now she's writing her memoirs."

Donna is working hard to bring the elderly of James Bay the social services that they need. The community development program for which she works is striving to give citizens of all ages a feeling of identity with the urban environment in which they live. This pilot program is developing activities which aid youth, families, and senior citizens, and which in turn generates a feeling of community responsibility on a neighbour-to-neighbour basis.

The next-door neighbour in Victoria can very well be full of surprises, as Leslie Drew, city editor of the *Victoria Colonist,* well knows. "We'll carry an article on ocean currents and the next day somebody will pop up who's an authority on ocean currents. A retired professor from South Africa, or someplace you'd least expect. Victoria is big enough – 200,000 including Sooke and the Saanich Peninsula – for anyone to find people with similar interests. Our daily notices reflect that. The esperanto speakers, the alpine rock gardeners, the UFO hunters all have their clubs. The B.C. tolerance for the bizarre is quite considerable. And yet we people out here don't move around Canada enough. We tend to sit complacently behind the screen of the Rockies. And similarly, they regard us as living on the edge of the plate."

There are those in Vancouver who think that Victorians live on the edge of the plate. The Gulf of Georgia separates these dissimilar urban worlds.

As one ferries across the gulf at day's end, the night-glow of Vancouver is sensed on the mainland coast.

Captain Anthony Ross describes it with conviction as "a magnificent harbour; you'd be very hard put to find anything in the world quite like it."

From his Centennial Dock tower, Harbourmaster Ross watches over the safety of Vancouver's waters and docks, and takes in the sound and light show that Vancouver mounts each dusk. Ski-lift lights on Grouse Mountain, West Vancouver commuters crossing the Lions Gate Bridge, dockside cranes silhouetted against the towering offices, and apartments aglow in the city. On the dock taxi wheels slowing in the rain, a harbour pilot skipping up the aluminum gangway of the Norwegian freighter *Fossganger,* clanking of closing hatches, linesmen's shouts, heavy hawsers slapping the hull and the haul-whine of winches. Tugs revving up, waters surging as the twenty-thousand-ton vessel backs away. The pilot established radio contact with the Port of Vancouver's controllers at the first narrows traffic centre.

"Vancouver Traffic, the *Fossganger.*"

"The *Fossganger,* Vancouver Traffic."

"There's a tug and tow leaving CPR crossing over to Vancouver Wharves' rail slip, there's a log boom outbound approaching Burnaby shoal. And a deep-sea ship has just departed Lynnterm Terminal."

And the *Fossganger* heads out of Burrard Inlet for Japan, joining the flow of vessels bearing the Canadian continent's potash, phosphates, coal, grain, sulphur, lumber, pulp and mineral concentrates.

"It's a very safe harbour indeed," Captain Ross in his precise British manner will tell you. "Now that the traffic centre radars are in operation, even the fogs aren't such a problem. Our controllers can talk a big grain carrier into the holding anchorage in the outer harbour much like an aircraft is talked down to the ground. During the summer months, when there are hundreds of yachts and motor-boats around here, we have a great big flashing red light just under the Lions Gate Bridge which lets small craft know when there's a dirty chop running outside. A strong flood tide with an east wind blowing against it kicks up a nasty confused little sea for a small boat. We get quite a few boats capsizing and somebody's got to go and fish them out. Now, the greater amount of small boatmen here have a lot of common sense, and some of them are most keen. But there is always some idiot who will not stick to the normal rules and behave like a civilized human being, and they are the ones who usually get into trouble."

Vancouver is a city in the fullest sense of the word. It's a place that journalist Jack Wasserman knows very well. He remembers the moment when "my father came out here on a business trip, looking for someone to sell insurance to. He arrived here in January, 1935, saw green grass on a golf course, and never went home to the prairies. This is coastal rain forest, jungle. He went scurrying around and found an apartment in the West End so that he would be within walking distance of Stanley Park and the water. He was just gassed by it. He was a prairie person. 'Gee, trees, big trees, water all around.'

"I went to Y camp as a kid. We went out on Howe Sound in what they called war canoes. Eight kids paddling with the whole centre of the canoe loaded with gear and we'd camp out, one, two, four nights. And we'd lie on the beach of Bowen Island – nobody around. You made your bed out of cedar boughs piled up high, you had a sleeping bag or a ground sheet and blankets. If it wasn't raining, you'd lie there and look at the sky, and if there was no moon, there'd be nothing but shooting stars everywhere because it was clear and it was beautiful and there wasn't any smog. Now I live ten minutes from town on a hill where there are wild animals, but I also look out on the harbour. On a clear day I can see Vancouver Island. I can't think of not being aware of the ocean."

But there are few people as keenly aware of the city as Jack. "Vancouver is my beat. If you're going to live in Canada, why would you live in Saskatoon or Oxbow? There are three places in Canada where everyone will move. Montreal, Toronto, and Vancouver. If people are going to starve anywhere in Canada, if there's a big depression, they'd rather starve here. At least it's warm. Here people will put up with a lot less. This isn't half the city that Toronto or Montreal is, in terms of the feeling, the action, the excitement that makes a city.

"But Vancouver swings. It's a big swinging town. It's a seaport. There's everything for everybody. We have naked ladies gyrating in cocktail bars, and we have rock bands and nice bands and shows coming into the Queen Elizabeth theatre and symphony. There's food for every taste, all the hedonistic experiences that are a form of show business."

Jack feels that the whole theory of the westward tilt applies in Canada as it does in America. "I don't know if all the nuts move here or if they become nuts once they're here. It's not because of the ocean, but because they're displaced from their roots. I think the people who are forced to move for a variety of reasons, they get to a new place and the phenomenon is fairly common. They don't have any roots, anything to hold on to. If you're by nature a lonely person, you'll be twice as lonely in a place where you don't know anybody to begin with."

One of Vancouver's antidotes for loneliness is Saturday night in a beer parlour. The sound may be country and western or Irish squeezebox, but the action is rather unchanging. There are the young new-to-town seeking each other, and the old familiars. And there's a whole flock who come down to Vancouver when the beer in Port Alberni or Gold River, Bella Coola or Prince Rupert begins to taste a bit flat.

M. Allerdale Grainger wrote *Woodsmen of the West* in 1912 and his words still describe the men who can be seen "drifting up the street to the Terminus and down the street to the Eureka, and having a drink with the crowd in the Columbia bar, and standing drinks to the girls at number so-and-so Dupont St. . . . If you are a woodsman, you will see fellow aristocrats who are going north to jobs: you maintain your elaborate knowledge of what is going on in the woods and where everyone is, and further, you know that in many a hotel and logging camp up the coast new arrivals from town will shortly be mentioning, casual-like: 'Jimmy Jones was down to the wharf. Been blowing her in great shape has Jimmy, round them saloons. Guess he'll be broke and hunting a job in another week, the pace he's going now.'"

One of modern Vancouver's great Sunday attractions is Canada's largest Chinatown. Its crowded sidewalks and jammed restaurants bear witness to the important ties Vancouver has with the Orient. Political posters in Chinese, English, Greek, and Italian grace shop windows, bearing witness to Canada's evolving ethnic base. Each new wave hopes that it can tell a story like that of Sing Fung, who owns a big Chinese provisions store on Pender Street.

"In the old country, they always said they would come to the Gold Mountain. That was its name. They came without their families and put in their work. Worked hard. No complaints. They did lots of things. They opened up land by hand, cleared the stumps, worked day and night. When they first came to Canada they worked in the mines, went logging, built the railways. They all made money, did better than they would have in the old country. My father worked all of his life here, and when I was four years old, we moved back to China. He bought lots of land in the fourth district of Canton when he went home. But when the Communists took over, he lost everything. I came back to Canada. I work hard, every day – ten days a week at least. I don't work eight hours a day, I work sixteen, seven days a week – maybe that's more than ten days. If you don't work that hard, you'll never make anything. But in Canada, if you make it, you'll keep it."

Sing Fung has more than a store. He owns a 600-acre farm in Surrey, twenty-two miles from Vancouver on the Fraser's flood plain. He fattens up a thousand head of steer and almost as many hogs, grows corn, grass, hay, and barley; and he has five sons.

Vancouver family stories come in all varieties. As Peter Cherniavsky, President of British Columbia Sugar Refining, Ltd., speaks of his grandfather, Forrest Rogers, one gains insight into the city's commercial history.

"Rogers was a young man working for American Sugar Refining in Brooklyn when he heard the railroad was going to come across Canada. So he went up to Montreal and saw the people who were putting the CPR together and he convinced them that what they needed was a little freight going west to east, because they would have lots going from east to west. The CPR fellows said, "If you're going out there, it might be something of interest to us." So a group of the fellows in the Bank of Montreal and the CPR took some shares in his company. When he came out here, there was tremendous pressure put on him to build in Victoria, but he was smart enough to realize that the growth would not be on an island, that it would eventually be on the mainland, somewhere near the terminus of the railway. Their first raw sugar was bought in Hong Kong, later it came from Fiji and Australia. That first refinery put through 50,000 pounds a day. Now we can do 2,000,000 pounds a day – all consumed in B.C."

The railroad ended in Gastown, the Burrard Inlet settlement named after garrulous hotel-keeper "Gassy Jack" Deighton, its founder. With the arrival of rail, Gastown became Vancouver. Its streets were paved and lit, and surrounded by elegant buildings. But time's passage moved the centre of activity and elegance away from Gastown, and by the 1960's it sat beside the railroad yard, a district of derelict buildings and down-on-their luck men.

One has to listen hard to Larry Killam when the switch engines pass by his office window. "Buildings like the one we are in were empty for fourteen years, no revenue of any kind. Now the revenues are phenomenal." Larry Killam and his associates are responsible for the resurrection and restoration of Gastown.

"What we had in Gastown was the great beginnings of a nice little ghetto, a festering area that could have consolidated itself and gone on to bigger things. In various areas of American cities, people actually become afraid of an area. They leave it to a confrontation between the police and the mavericks down there. The restoration and promotion of Gastown nipped it in the bud. There was no second location for it to start in Vancouver. I don't think people realize what the sociological significance of this restoration is.

"Our primary interest was to buy old buildings – we own ten – and have all the groovy things be a beacon in the night for all the people trying to do groovy things. We renovated them with amateur labour and young enthusiasts. The Gastown of today gives people of the Lower Mainland their old-town antiquity. It's been well enough done, it's genuine, it hasn't been faked up. They don't have to be ashamed of the place. It's not a tourist trap. Prices on a variety of merchandise and foods down here are quite reasonable. It's a fairly enviable concentration; no huge thing, but we did save our original historical core. I'd hope that the same level of concern and aesthetics and environmental awareness that we concentrated in this area – not the same formulas or anything – could be useful in another way. It's a gargantuan project, but I would like to see our whole country tidied up."

Amongst those who are trying to ensure that the Lower Mainland area of British Columbia does not become more of a mess to be tidied up is Walter Hardwick. Professor in Urban Planning at the University of British Columbia, he has served as an alderman on Vancouver's City Council and is currently active in regional planning. He points to new inner city parks and marinas along Vancouver's False Creek – both the result of Canadian Pacific's Project 200 – as steps in the right direction. The recent zoning of 76,000 acres on the Fraser River's flood plain as agricultural land is another effort to preserve this densely populated region's ecological balance.

"The simple fact of the matter," Hardwick has observed, "is that land is nailed down as greenbelt. From the planner's viewpoint we've created a livable region. Now that means permitting growth as unobtrusively as possible. We're going to do what we can to strengthen the regional towncentres, so that more people can live closer to their places of work. By that, we don't mean creating shopping centres that cater to the automobile, nor do we mean industrial parks, because they've failed miserably as a work place. Our idea is to take areas like New Westminster and Burnaby, identify major corporations that can be moved into offices in these areas, put up lots of multiple housing there to accommodate the girls who are coming in for secretarial work, create transportation connections between these regional towncentres and the airport, and a whole lot of other strategic things. This is already underway: British Columbia Telephone for instance has moved its headquarters to Burnaby, and there are others. This is all designed to keep these areas viable, livable, and cut the major long-distance cross-commuters. And I think this

should be able to help us keep the scale of living where we have it right now."

For people like Nina Wheaton, the scale was always too large. She had to come to Vancouver from Campbell River, for training as a nurse. The training in the city was undertaken to ensure her a good job on the outer coast. As a child, she spent a year with her father when he was keeper of the Quatsino Light at Vancouver Island's northern end. "I like going down to the sea when it's really stormy. You really can't do that in Vancouver. At Quatsino, it was so neat, it was stormy so much of the time. You could go out alone, and there were just great expanses. When you're down by the sea, everything else gets blown out of your mind. You can be feeling really bad or be happy, whatever. It's just blown out of your mind, and it's just peaceful."

For those whose years will not be lived on the outer coast, Murray Newman offers the Vancouver Aquarium in Stanley Park. Newman's vivid appreciation of his coast has given birth to the vital displays of Vancouver's "Temple of the Fish". As its founding director, he has attempted to recreate not only underwater environments, but also a sense of the incredibly exciting intertidal zone created by steady seasonal rains and giant tides that range fifteen feet. The tropics cannot match the British Columbia intertidal zone, for the equatorial sun sterilizes the margin of the sea. Only under water does the tropical explorer find a world magically alive.

"I've dived in Bora Bora, the Great Barrier Reef, the Indian Ocean, and Ceylon. The British Columbia coast matches any of them – it's the most under-rated area for diving in the world. Deep olives and maroon reds, and the range of fishes – from tiny neutobranches who prance around like belly dancers to wolf eels and rock fishes – red, yellow, and green."

Population along the coast between Vancouver and Prince Rupert has not grown in the last decades. More and more, the processing of the yield of sea and forest is being done on the shores of the Gulf of Georgia. Amongst the people one once might have found permanently stationed in a small coastal settlement are Fisheries Service researchers from the Federal Department of the Environment. When they're not on field trips, they're in Vancouver, working up their reports and comparing notes. One particular dialogue reflects issues now being faced by residents of these shores. Listen to their conversation, and know that it will continue.

"I don't know why the government has never supported small communities along the coast. Thirty years from now they really should have a coastal road from Prince Rupert to Vancouver, with ferries across the inlets, like in Norway. In Alaska, there are plenty of small coastal towns, and good reason to have year-round car ferries. But that isn't the case here yet."

"You could say we like it as it is."

"Well, I don't. The B.C. Coast isn't friendly."

"The fact that it's a water wilderness isn't tragic to me."

"Well it is when you think that your neighbours never get the opportunity to go where you go, and you would never go there if you didn't work for the fisheries."

"My neighbours couldn't care less – they have no desire to go where I go."

"Because they've never been there."

*"There'll always be a Victoria, with its splendid Front Street,
There'll always be an Empress, where past and present meet."*

Solemn Christmas prayers honour those who died in distant wars. Victoria veterans recall their resistance in Hong Kong.

Boxing Day sets two sides a-scrumming in Victoria, polar bears a-dipping and "bathtubbers" a-voyaging in Nanaimo.

Racing into blustery winds on the Straits of Juan de Fuca, yachtsmen from the whole Pacific coast head for the lightship that gave its name to the event – Swiftsure.

Vancouver must be the fastest growing ninety-year-old on the North American continent. Canada's largest port city, she ranks third in population – over a million inhabitants. Residents and visitors enjoy her access to wilderness; Canada profits by her access to Asia.

A Japan-bound cargo of Saskatchewan wheat, a barge-load of steel just off a Russian freighter; the port is on the go, sending out coal, potash, sulphur, and lumber for the world's finished goods.

Stanley Park's Lost Lagoon is a habitat for both Royal Swans and migrating waterfowl. The shores of English Bay are a meeting ground for Canadians come west for a new life.

Gardens that bloom from Easter to Thanksgiving are only part of the special "climate" that has drawn so many from the East.

Vancouver has Canada's largest Chinese community. Their forebearers worked in the gold-fields and built the railroads. On a Sunday, Pender Street is alive with families who have come to shop and dine.

Sikhs from Punjab play Kabaddi *by tagging an opponent, eluding tacklers, and sprinting for centrefield. Their continuous cry, "Kabaddi," proves they have done it all in one breath.*

At the Pacific National Exhibition, woodsmen demonstrate the skills that conquered a wilderness. In Stanley Park, Dogwood blooms in spring. Strength and grace each have their place.

City dwellers sense
The setting sun,
And follow it
To the shores beyond.